W9-BEQ-338

DANCERS

THE PERFORMERS

Laura Conlon

The Rourke Press, Inc.
Vero Beach, Florida 32964

Edited by Sandra A. Robinson

PHOTO CREDITS
© Emil Punter/Photo Vision: cover, title page, pages 4, 8, 13, 15, 18;
© Fred Lyon: page 17; courtesy Puerto Rico Office of Tourism: page 7;
courtesy Ballet Theatre Pennsylvania: pages 10, 12, 21

ACKNOWLEDGMENTS
The author thanks the Bonnie Ardelean Dance Studio (Aurora, IL)
and the Geneva (IL) Park District's Sunset Park for their assistance in
the preparation of photographs for this book

Library of Congress Cataloging-in-Publication Data

Conlon, Laura, 1959-
    Dancers / Laura Conlon.
    p. cm. — (The Performers discovery library)
    Includes index.
    ISBN 1-57103-064-6
    1. Dancing—Juvenile literature. 2. Dancers—Juvenile literature.
[1. Dancers. 2. Vocational guidance. 3. Occupations.] I. Title.
II. Series.
GV1596.5.C66   1994
792.8—dc20
                                                        94-12387
                                                        CIP
Printed in the USA   AC

TABLE OF CONTENTS

DANCERS

People around the world love to watch the grace and beauty of dancers. Dancers show feelings and ideas through their movements. Sometimes they tell a story in their dance.

People who become dancers love what they do. Dancing is hard work. Dancers have to practice every day. Their hard work pays off when the music begins, the lights go up — and the dancers step onto the stage!

Dancers learn to show feelings and ideas using movements

KINDS OF DANCERS

Ballet is one of the oldest forms of dance. A ballet usually tells a story. Ballet dancers learn very special steps and body positions.

Tap dancers wear special shoes with metal pieces on the bottom. Tap dancers "tap" their feet to the music.

Folk dancers perform dances from long ago. Each type of folk dance has special costumes.

Modern, jazz and acrobatic are a few of the other types of dancers. Some dancers may also perform in musicals.

Folk dancers perform dances from long ago

LEARNING TO BE A DANCER

Dancers usually begin training when they are children. Most beginning dancers study ballet. They go to special dance schools. Dancers can also take dance classes in some colleges.

Dancers may later study with dance companies, or groups. Dance companies prepare students to become **professional** dancers. There they work very hard and take classes every day.

Most beginning dancers study ballet

DIRECTION

A dancer does not work alone.

A **choreographer** chooses the music and creates the movements — steps — for a dance. The choreographer teaches the dancer the steps.

The "dance master" watches **rehearsal,** or practice, and makes sure the dancer's movements are correct.

A professional dance company has a "director" who chooses the dances and the dancers who will perform them.

After many rehearsals, professional dancers of the Ballet Theatre Pennsylvania perform Dracula

Dancing demands strength and balance

PRACTICE MAKES PERFECT

Dancers usually begin practice at the **barre,** a wooden bar attached to a wall. There, they warm up and stretch their muscles. They practice special steps and body positions.

After warm-up the dancers go to the "center," where they learn and practice the steps of the dances they will perform.

Even the world's greatest dancers practice every day.

Dancers begin practice at a wooden rail called a barre

COSTUMES AND MAKEUP

Dance costumes are different for each type of dance. Ballet dancers wear tight-fitting leotards. Ballerinas, female ballet dancers, wear special "pointe shoes" to dance on tiptoe. A ballerina may wear a beautiful skirt called a "tutu."

Because stage lights are very bright, some dancers wear makeup so that they won't look pale. They may also wear makeup to help them look like a special character — even an animal!

Dancers of the San Francisco Ballet perform the Nutcracker Suite *under bright stage lights*

A DANCER'S WORKPLACE

Practice rooms usually have wooden floors, a practice barre, and a large mirror so that dancers can watch their movements. A piano stands nearby so that the dancers can practice to music.

Dancers perform on a platform called a **stage.** The stage can be empty or filled with **scenery.** The choreographer usually chooses a "stage designer" who creates scenery for the dance.

Young dancers compete on a wooden stage

ONSTAGE

After many rehearsals, the dancers are ready to perform. Waiting to go onstage, the dancers stretch their muscles. They check their makeup and costumes. They put powder called rosin on the bottoms of their shoes so that they won't slip onstage. The curtain rises, the music starts, and the dance begins in front of an **audience.**

Dancers in a professional company may perform five or six times a week. Sometimes they perform in many different cities.

These are members of the Ballet Theatre Pennsylvania in a stage perfomance of Dracula

CAREERS IN DANCE

Dancing is a difficult profession, or job. Dancers always face the risk of hurting themselves. Dancing jobs are hard to find. Many dancers try out — but there are only a few jobs. Dancers sometimes become choreographers or dance teachers.

Most people who love to dance don't choose it as a career. However, they often keep dancing with dance groups in their communities.

Glossary

audience (AW dee ents) — a group of people gathered to see a performance

ballet (baa LAY) — a type of dance based on special steps and performed to music; it sometimes tells a story

barre (BAR) — a wooden bar on the wall that dancers hold on to while practicing

choreographer (kor e AH gruh fer) — a person who plans the movements — steps — of a dance

professional (pro FESH uh nul) — a person who is trained and paid for doing a job

rehearsal (re HER suhl) — practice for a future performance

scenery (SEE ner ee) — painted screens, hangings and objects used onstage to help audiences imagine a certain place

stage (STAYDJ) — the part of the theater where the performance takes place

INDEX